THE ELECTROMAGNETIC SPECTRUM

UNDERSTANDING AND USING X-RAYS

ELIZABETH RUBIO

Enslow PUBLISHING

Published in 2022 by Enslow Publishing, LLC.
101 W. 23rd Street, Suite 240, New York, NY 10011

Library of Congress Cataloging-in-Publication Data

Names: Rubio, Elizabeth, author.
Title: Understanding and using X-rays / Elizabeth Rubio.
Description: New York : Enslow Publishing, 2022. | Series: The electromagnetic spectrum | Audience: Grades 7 to 12. | Includes bibliographical references and index.
Identifiers: LCCN 2019015484| ISBN 9781978515017 (library bound) | ISBN 9781978515000 (pbk.)
Subjects: LCSH: X-rays—Juvenile literature. | Electromagnetic waves—Juvenile literature.
Classification: LCC QC481 .R83 2022 | DDC 539.7/222—dc23
LC record available at https://lccn.loc.gov/2019015484

Printed in the United States of America

To Our Readers: We have done our best to make sure all websites in this book were active and appropriate when we went to press. However, the author and the publisher have no control over and assume no liability for the material available on those websites or on any websites they may link to. Any comments or suggestions can be sent by email to customerservice@enslow.com.

Photos Credits: Cover Cultura RM Exclusive/PhotoStock-Israel/Getty Image; p. 5 NASA/CXC/IAFE/G.Dubner et al & ESA/XMM-Newton; p. 8 VectorMine /Shutterstock.com; p. 9 Designua/Shutterstock.com; p. 12 Universal Images Group/Getty Images; p. 15 Davide Palermo/Alamy Stock Photo; p. 17 Wellcome Images/Wikimedia Commons/File: V0029523.jpg/CC BY 4.0. ; p. 19 Science History Images/Alamy Stock Photo; p. 22 Universal Images Group/Getty Images; p. 24 fmajor/E+/Getty Images; p. 25 Mark Kostich/E+/Getty Images; p. 29 Bill Oxford/E+/Getty Images; p. 32 RayArt Graphics/Alamy Stock Photo; p. 35 Fastfission/Wikimedia Commons/File: Fission bomb assembly methods.svg /Public Domain; p. 39 Rena Schild/Shutterstock.com; p. 43 NASA; p. 46 dpa picture alliance/Alamy Stock Photo; p. 49 Dino Fracchia/Alamy Stock Photo; p. 52 Painting/Alamy Stock Photo (landscape); p. 52 Historic Images/Alamy Stock Photo (portrait); p. 54 Berkut_34/iStock/Getty Images; cover background, interior pages (faceted color pattern) s_maria/Shutterstock.com; interior pages (wave graphic) MagicMary/Shutterstock.com.

CONTENTS

INTRODUCTION

What comes to mind when you think of X-rays? Most likely, you think of a black-and-white picture of someone's bones. Maybe you've even had X-rays taken yourself.

Pictures like that are indeed a very common use of X-rays. However, they are not the only medical use of X-rays. Moreover, X-rays have many uses besides those in medicine.

X-rays have existed for all time, but humans only discovered them in the late nineteenth century. Human use of X-rays only dates back to the late nineteenth century. In the short time since then, humans have used X-rays to examine everything from microscopic molecules to faraway galaxies.

Although most X-rays in the universe occur naturally, these cosmic X-rays generally do not reach the surface of Earth. Earth is shielded from cosmic X-rays by its ionosphere, which is the outer layer of Earth's atmosphere. Here on Earth's surface, X-rays are generated by human-made devices, such as the machines used to take X-ray photographs of bones and teeth.

It is lucky all the cosmic X-rays reflect off Earth's atmosphere because X-rays can be harmful. Too much exposure to X-rays can cause damage, some of which can last a lifetime. When X-rays were first discovered, this fact was not yet understood. Many people became sick and some even died before scientists realized the harm X-rays could cause. Today, anyone who is exposed to X-rays, including patients, is carefully monitored to ensure they do not receive too high a dose.

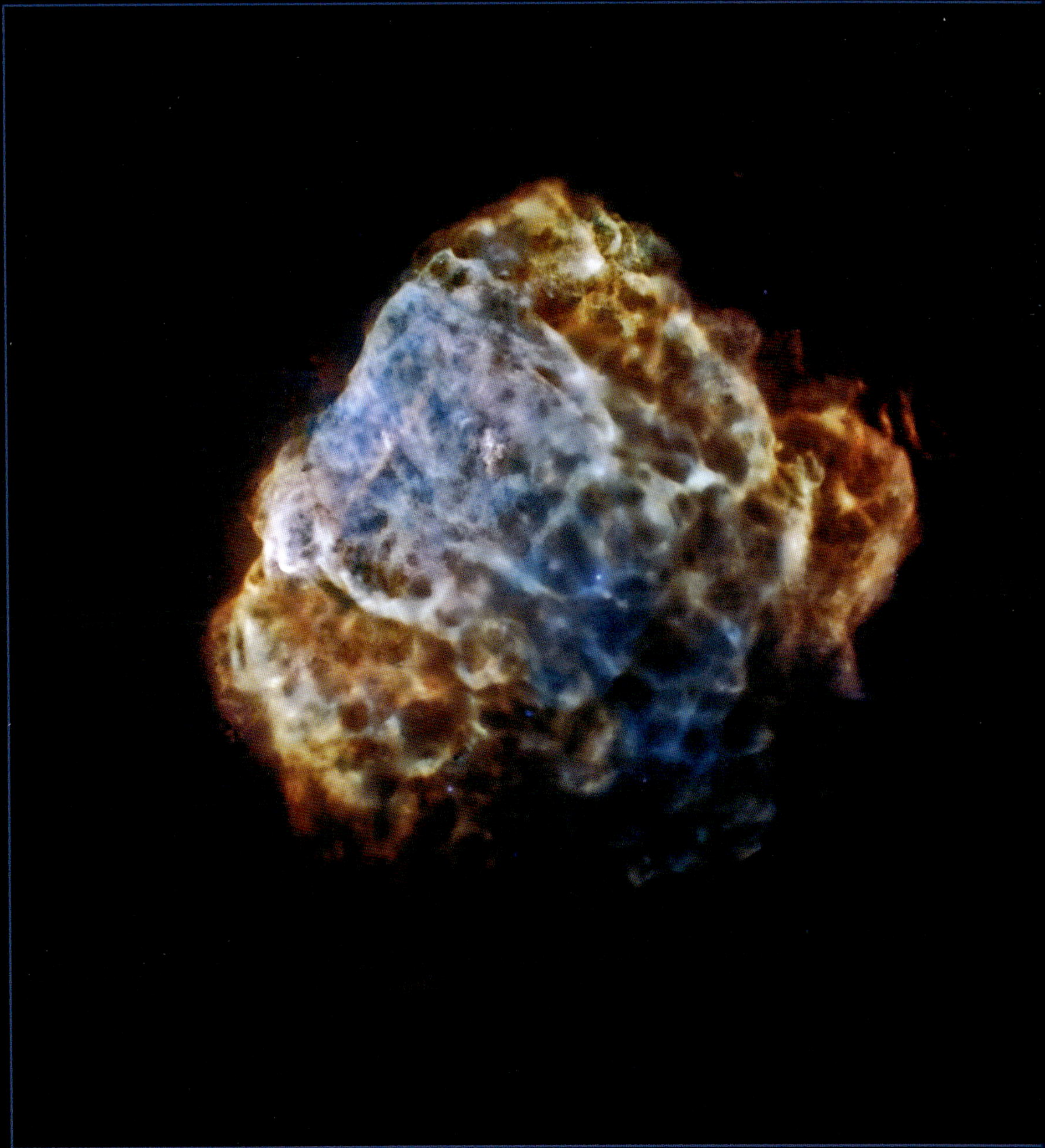

This image is an X-ray photo of a supernova 7,000 light-years from Earth. Low-energy X-rays are colored red, medium-energy X-rays are colored green, and high-energy X-rays are colored blue.

X-rays are not used just for medicine. Scientists also examine the X-rays emitted by stars and galaxies. This helps them discover new stars and learn more about the stars that are visible.

X-rays are also used to examine small molecules. The ways X-rays interact with crystals allow scientists to figure out how the atoms in a crystal are arranged. They can then understand the shape of any single repeating unit of a crystal, such as a strand of DNA. In fact, this is how the double-helix shape of DNA was discovered.

X-rays have more sinister uses as well. The power of X-rays is instrumental in the explosion of a nuclear bomb. X-rays are also produced by nuclear bombs upon detonation. Nuclear bombs are the most devastating weapons humans have created. Research into their development began almost as soon as X-rays were discovered. Many people favor ending all development and stockpiling of nuclear weapons, but so far, this has not occurred.

Not all uses of X-rays are medical or scientific. X-rays are also used in security screening, such as the scanners through which luggage passes at airports. X-rays can be used to detect forgeries in art, money, and electronics. They can also be used to check for breaks or defects in infrastructure, such as pipes, railroads, and bridges. All these uses keep people safe and secure.

In just over one hundred years, humanity has harnessed the power of X-rays, for both benefit and harm. People will likely continue to find new uses for this powerful form of light in the years to come.

THE ELECTROMAGNETIC SPECTRUM

CHAPTER ONE

X-rays are a form of light. All light is part of the electromagnetic spectrum. Another term for light is electromagnetic radiation. X-rays are electromagnetic radiation that is more energetic than visible light. X-rays are not visible, but that doesn't mean they don't exist.

What Is the Electromagnetic Spectrum?

The electromagnetic spectrum includes the entire range of all types of electromagnetic radiation. This radiation includes all forms of light—not only X-rays, but also visible light, ultraviolet and infrared light, microwaves, radio waves, and gamma rays. Light is also called electromagnetic radiation because it is a wave of alternating electric and magnetic fields. Just like water in a lake when you drop a stone into the water, light travels in waves, spreading out in all directions from its source.

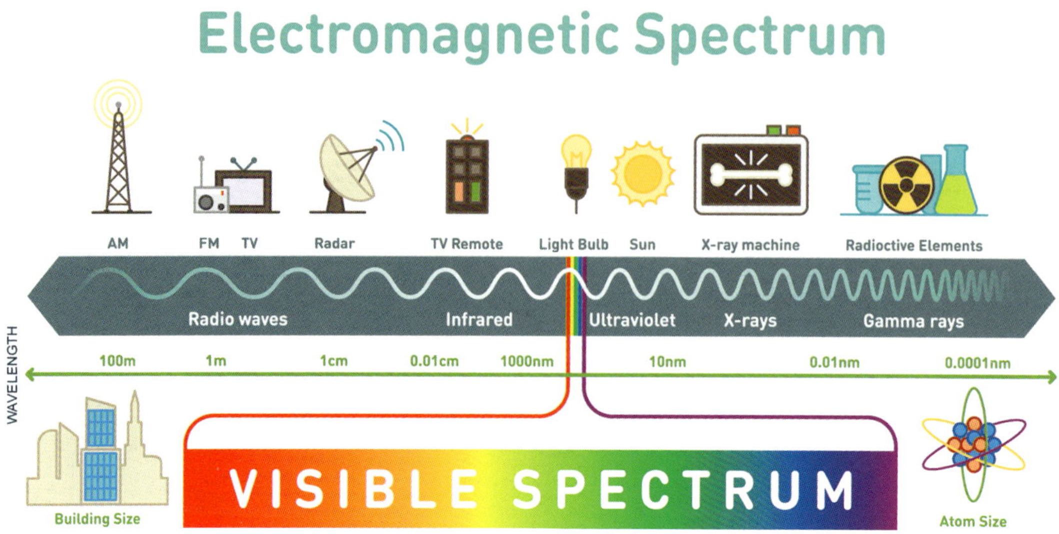

The electromagnetic spectrum encompasses all electromagnetic energy. X-rays are near the right end of the spectrum shown in this image because they have a lot of energy.

All types of light are waves, so each type of light has a specific wavelength. A wavelength is the distance between two crests of a wave. Light with shorter wavelengths has more energy than light with longer wavelengths. Put another way, light with shorter wavelengths is more powerful and can penetrate more objects than light with longer wavelengths.

Wavelengths in the electromagnetic spectrum range from thousands of kilometers on the low-energy end of the spectrum to 1×10^{-13} meters on the high-energy end. So, the lowest energy light has a wavelength longer than a country, and the highest energy light has a wavelength smaller than the diameter of an atom.

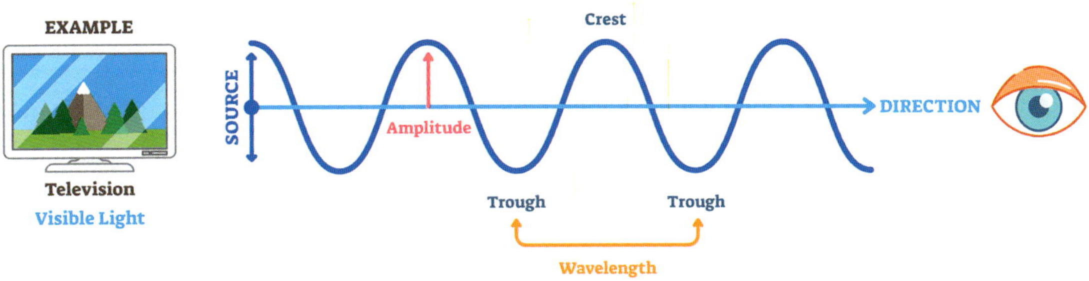

Amplitude is the height of the wave, measured as half the distance from the trough to the crest. Wavelength is the distance between crests or troughs.

How Do X-Rays Compare to Other Types of Electromagnetic Radiation?

X-rays have shorter wavelengths than most other forms of light. They encompass wavelengths from 0.1 to 10 nanometers (nm).[1] One nanometer is one-millionth of a millimeter, the shortest measurement on a metric ruler. The nanometer scale is much, much smaller than can be seen with the naked eye. For example, the common bacterium *Escherechia coli* is about 1,000 nm long. That's much longer than even the longest X-rays.

X-rays also have more energy than electromagnetic radiation with longer wavelengths, including visible light. This characteristic means they can move through objects that absorb visible light. This property of X-rays makes them very useful in medical imaging. X-rays can pass through soft tissues, such as skin and muscle, before reflecting off of bone. In contrast, visible light reflects off of skin.

What Is Ionizing Radiation?

The high energy of X-rays means they can interact in special ways with matter. X-rays, along with gamma rays and ultraviolet radiation, are called ionizing radiation. This means they can cause electrons to be ejected from matter when they strike that matter's surface. This loss of electrons gives the matter a positive charge. Molecules with a charge of any kind are called ions. Thus, ionizing radiation creates ions.

Unlike nonionizing radiation, such as light and radio waves, ionizing radiation can be harmful to living things. Ions within living tissue can cause damage to cells and can even disrupt the genetic code itself. This can lead to illness.

However, ionizing radiation occurs naturally across the universe. All living things are exposed to some amount of ionizing radiation. They have thus evolved mechanisms for protecting against the damage it can inflict. Only amounts of ionizing radiation too high for living systems to protect against result in harm to people.

The harmful effects of ionizing radiation on the body vary. In the short term, they can include burns, as well as damage to major body systems such as the nervous system, the digestive system, and the immune system. In the long term, they can include cancer, infertility, cataracts, and hereditary effects. Hereditary effects means that the future children of a person who has had an exposure may have deformities. Importantly, long-term effects may arise without short-term effects having been present. For example, it is possible for a person to develop skin cancer without ever having had a sunburn.

RADIOISOTOPES

Much of the ionizing radiation that occurs naturally comes from radioisotopes. These are atoms that have an unstable atomic composition, which causes them to decay into different atoms over time. For example, carbon-14 is a radioisotope of carbon that decays quite slowly into nitrogen-14, a nonradioactive atom.

Radioisotopes emit different kinds of radiation, depending on how they decay. X-rays are usually emitted along with another type of radiation. This other type of radiation may be gamma rays, or it may be small particles. These are called alpha particles and beta particles.

The International Commission on Radiological Protection (ICRP) is an independent, international organization devoted to assessing and promoting safety regarding ionizing radiation. This organization has determined the maximum amount of radiation a person can receive in a given time and still be safe. An exposure in a specific time is called a dose. Various measurements exist for radiation doses. Common units used for human doses are rem (in the United States) and sievert (international). Other units include rads and roentgens.

Crucially, living things can withstand higher doses if the length of exposure is short. Over longer periods, higher doses become problematic. This is the reason it is acceptable for a patient to receive a single X-ray scan, while the X-ray technician must remain outside the room or behind a safe wall. Because

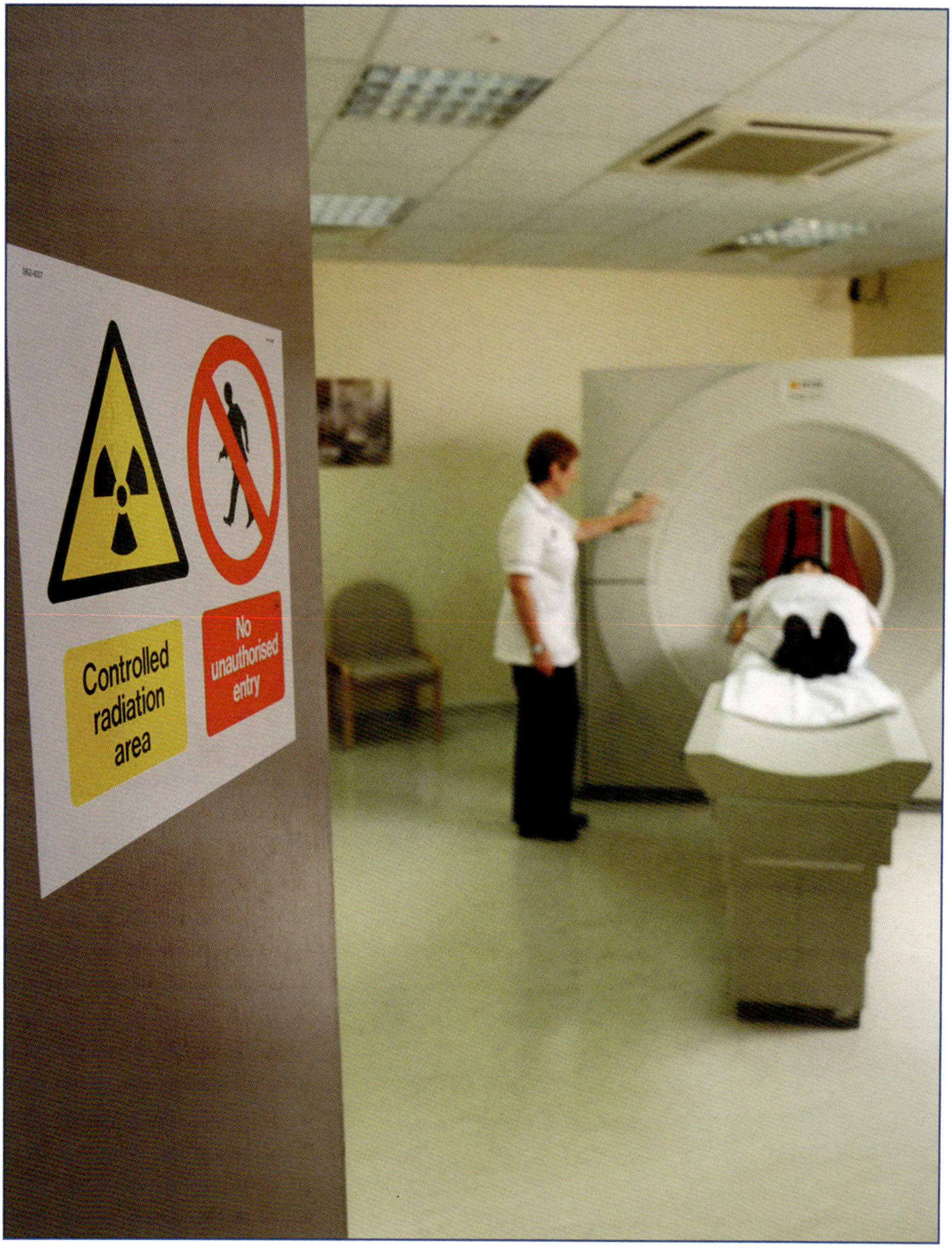

X-rays can be harmful to living things, so places where X-rays are used must have limited access. People should monitor how much radiation they are exposed to and limit unnecessary exposure.

the X-ray technician must administer many X-ray scans every day, he or she must be protected from high doses of radiation. The patient will not receive X-ray scans every day, so a single dose is safe.

Protection from a source of radiation takes the form of shielding and distance. Shielding refers to placing material between the person and the source of radiation. This material absorbs the radiation, preventing it from reaching the person. Shielding for X-rays is often a heavy metal, such as lead. Distance also protects against radiation. Radiation spreads out in all directions from its source, so far away, the effects are not as strong. As an analogy, think of one flashlight right in front of your face and one a mile away. The one right in front of your face appears extremely bright, while the one a mile away is very dim. The same principle is true for radiation. X-rays are, after all, just a form of light.

CHAPTER TWO

THE HISTORY OF X-RAYS

X-rays, like every other type of electromagnetic radiation, have always existed. Yet humans did not recognize them until very late in the nineteenth century. This was a very exciting time for research into electromagnetic radiation, as many of the invisible forms of light, such as radio waves, X-rays, and gamma rays, were beginning to be recognized and understood.

The Cathode-Ray Tube

The mid- to late nineteenth century saw a great deal of experimentation with electricity. This new phenomenon fascinated scientists and engineers. It promised to hold the keys to understanding a great deal about the physical universe. It soon became clear that electricity, magnetism, and light were all somehow related. But more research was needed to fully unlock the secrets of these phenomena.

A cathode-ray tube (CRT) is a glass vacuum tube with electrodes inside. When voltage is applied across the electrodes, electrons move between them, causing the tube to glow.

Cathode rays were a major part of this research. A cathode ray is a beam of electrons that can be observed inside a vacuum tube. To study these rays, researchers used cathode-ray tubes (CRTs). To make a CRT, a positive electrode is positioned at one end of a glass tube and a negative electrode is positioned at the other. All gas is removed from the tube. Then it is sealed, which forms a vacuum. When a voltage is applied across the electrode, a beam of electrons moves through the tube, creating a glow.

As scientists experimented with CRTs, they began to notice odd effects they could not explain. When the voltage was high enough, odd things happened. Strange effects could be seen on nearby objects. It seemed some sort of matter or energy was escaping the tubes and affecting the area around them. This was especially noticeable if any photographic film was nearby. In fact, some researchers deliberately experimented with CRTs and photographic film, producing photos taken in complete darkness. The photos showed fuzzy images of objects placed between the CRT and the film.[1] These researchers did not realize they were taking X-ray photographs.

CATHODE-RAY TUBES IN SCREENS

Although the cathode-ray tube was instrumental in discovering X-rays, that is not what it is most famous for. Cathode-ray tubes were used for decades in glowing screens, such as television and computer screens. These screens were called CRTs because of their use of cathode-ray tubes.

CRT screens were gradually replaced with lighter, more efficient technologies, such as LEDs, LCDs, and plasma. Yet CRTs dominated the technology market for decades before the newer technologies were even developed.

Wilhelm Röntgen used X-rays to take this photo of his wife's hand. The bones and her wedding ring are clearly visible. This photograph showed the possibilities of the use of X-rays in medicine.

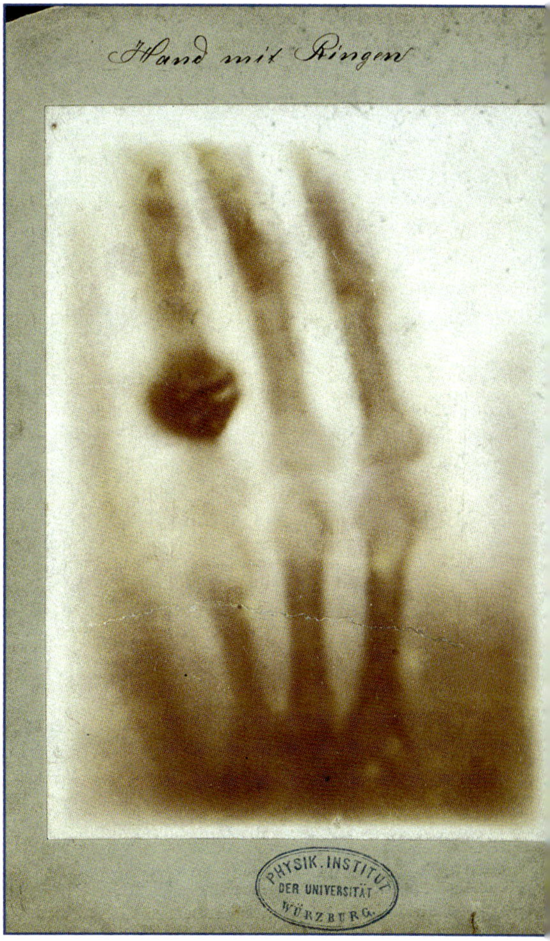

Röntgen and the Discovery of X-Rays

German physicist Wilhelm Röntgen was keen to learn what was coming out of CRTs. He began studying the rays emitted by these tubes when high voltage was applied. He didn't fully understand the rays, so he called them "X." In 1895, he published a paper about these mysterious "X" rays. X-rays got their name from his use of the term.[2] For this reason, one measurement of a radiation dose, a roentgen, is named after him.

Röntgen noticed the mysterious rays could pass through objects such as cardboard and even books and papers on his desk. He began deliberately using the rays to take photographs of objects. At first, he photographed objects in his office. Then, one day, he took a photograph of his wife's hand using the rays. He and his wife were both startled to see the photo showed her bones and her wedding ring, but not her skin or muscles.

Röntgen immediately recognized the use such photography could have for medicine. He wrote letters to physicians all across Europe, encouraging them to experiment with "shadowgrams," as he called them. The recipients of his letters took their own X-ray photographs, and word spread to more medical professionals. Soon, doctors across the world were making medical breakthroughs thanks to the new technology.

The Rise of Radiography

Röntgen's discovery led to a flurry of research in medical radiography. Right away, doctors began using X-rays to take photographs of their own bones and the bones of their patients. But many were not satisfied with still photographs. Complicating matters, at the time it took over an hour to take an X-ray photo, during which the subject might be in considerable pain and had to stay absolutely still. Some subjects, victims of gunshot wounds or other traumatic damage, did not have an hour to spare.

Many scientists, including Röntgen himself, built devices to show X-ray images in real time. To achieve this goal, they coated screens with fluorescent materials. These materials lit up, emitting visible light, when excited by X-rays. American scientist Thomas Edison invented a "Vitascope," a mass-produced real-time X-ray device, which later became known as a fluoroscope. This device relied on fluorescent screens to produce a real-time X-ray image. It could show doctors exactly what was happening inside a person's body as it happened. Fluoroscopes are still in use in medicine today.

This photo shows Thomas Edison examining Clarence Dally's hand using a fluoroscope. Edison designed and built this fluoroscope.

Although the interest and research in X-ray photography was initially substantial, people involved in the research began to become ill and even die. A man who worked for Thomas Edison, Clarence Madison Dally, took regular X-ray photographs of his hands. He soon developed such severe cancer on his hands that both his arms had to be amputated. This was not enough to save him, however—he died of cancer not long after. His was the first known death as a result of X-ray exposure.[3]

Other scientists and doctors—experimenting with X-rays, demonstrating their use, or treating patients—began to notice that the body parts examined under X-rays often developed burns and hair loss. Sometimes the affected body part would swell and blister, leaving the patient in terrible pain. These effects could last for weeks. It became clear that the burns, hair loss, blistering, swelling, and cancer were direct effects of exposure to X-rays. A safer method of X-ray imaging was needed.

Serbian American physicist Mihajlo Pupin improved Edison's fluoroscope by coating the fluorescent screen in a different substance.[4] This reduced the time an exposure required from an hour or more to only a few minutes. This substantial decrease in exposure time made X-ray imaging far safer. Thanks to this and other breakthroughs, X-rays became quite safe, taking only moments for exposure to be sufficient. Illnesses and deaths decreased, and the use of X-rays in medical imaging became the widespread application known today.

CHAPTER THREE

MEDICAL USES OF X-RAYS

By far, the most widely known use of X-rays is medical imaging. You yourself have quite possibly had an X-ray photograph or two taken of your bones or teeth. X-ray imaging can show broken or deformed bones, dense masses of tissue or material, and other internal structures in a completely noninvasive way.

How Radiography Works

The use of X-rays or other radioactive materials to produce images is called radiography. Radiography encompasses all images produced using radiation, including those made using sources besides X-rays (some images use gamma rays or radioactive particles rather than X-rays).

Regardless of the type of radiation used or the exact process involved, all radiography works in a similar manner. A beam of radiation is directed at a subject. An absorptive surface or screen is placed on the opposite side of the subject. As the beam passes through the subject, some of the waves are absorbed, while others pass through the subject. All the waves that pass completely through the subject strike the absorptive surface on the other side of the subject. This surface can be either film or a digital receptor. The varying intensities of the radiation that makes it all the way through the subject to the absorptive surface produce the image. Lighter and darker areas show the structures of the subject. This is exactly the same way that black and white photography works with visible light, except that visible light is reflected off a surface, while X-rays are absorbed by it.

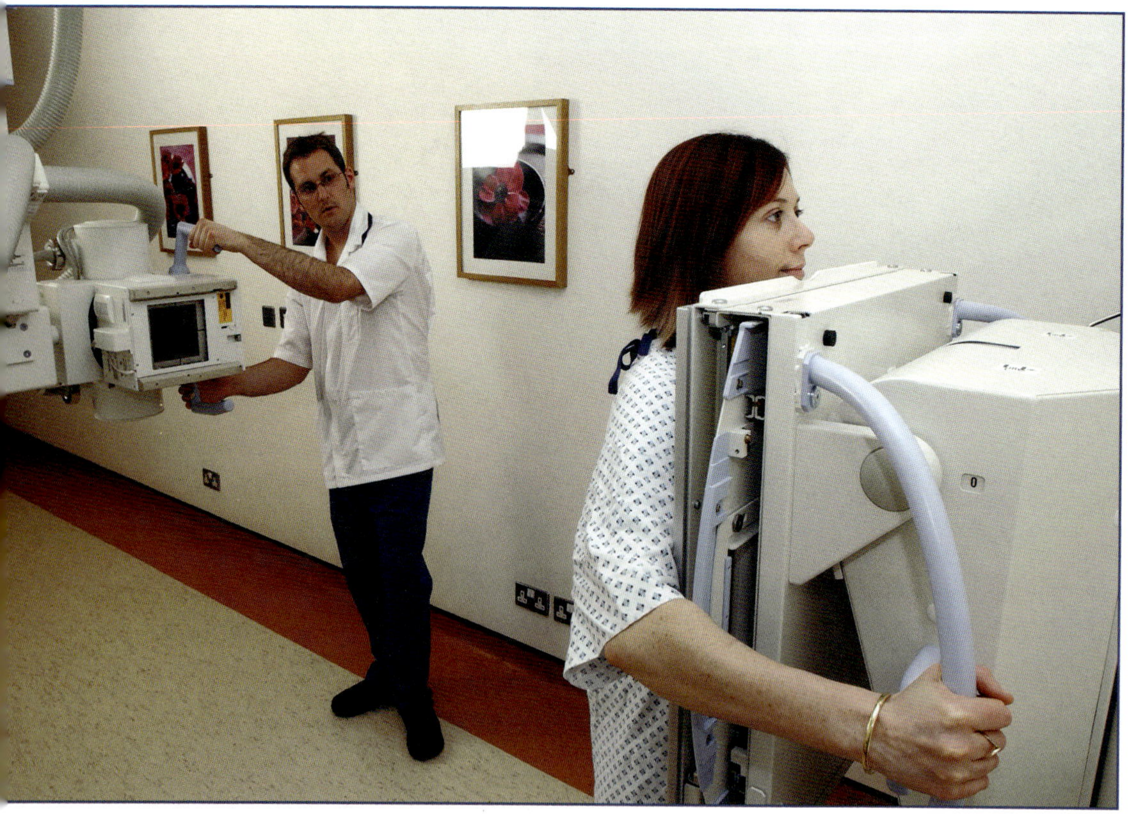

The X-ray technician stands beside the source of the X-rays. The patient stands in front of the detector screen. The X-rays will pass through the person onto the screen.

Some radiographic images are still, while others may be moving images. Moving images may be captured on video so they can be reviewed as necessary. Today, most images are rendered digitally, although physical copies, such as X-ray films, may still be used in some applications.

Types and Uses of Medical X-Rays

There are many types of medical radiography, and they have myriad uses.

The basic X-ray image, a two-dimensional still image, is very widely used. In the medical field, this is known as projection radiography. This type of radiography can be used to diagnose bone fractures, pneumonia, heart failure, collapsed lungs, bowel obstruction, and bone alignment, among other conditions. It is also an early tool in the detection of cancer.[1]

A computed tomography, or CT, scan (sometimes called computed axial tomography, or CAT scan), uses a computer along with a beam of X-rays to produce a cross-sectional image of body structures.[2] This imaging technique can precisely differentiate structures of varying density. This makes it so that not only hard tissues, such as bones, are visible but also soft tissues, such as muscles and blood vessels. For this reason, CT scans have a wide variety of medical applications, including detection of tumors and investigation of abnormal soft tissues such as the heart and brain. CT scans are sometimes aided by the addition of a material such as iodine. The X-rays used in the scan cause structures with large amounts of iodine to appear different in the image, making structures such as blood vessels easier to see.

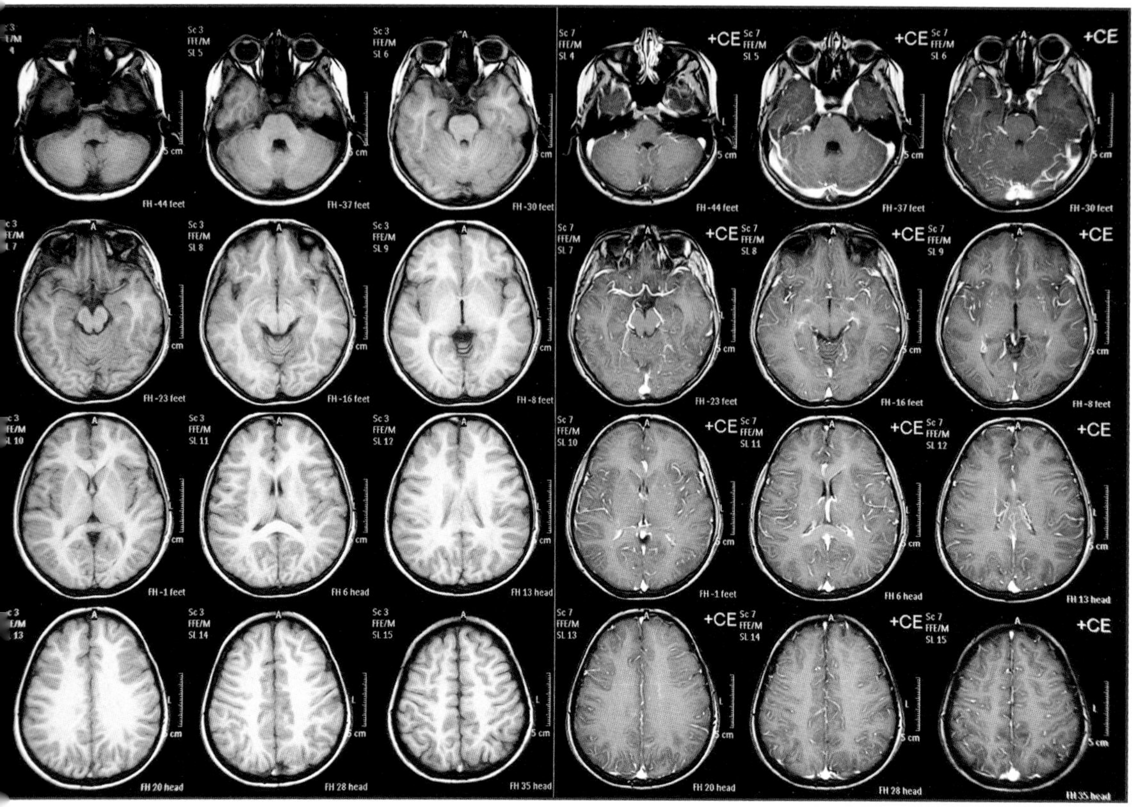

These images were taken using computed tomography (CT). The images show layers of the skull and brain of a child. Doctors use CT scans like these to examine tissues for damage and disease.

The use of these materials is called contrast because it makes the structures they fill show up brightly on the scan.

Dual energy X-ray absorptiometry (DEXA) is a technique that uses two beams of X-rays emitted perpendicular to each other that are scanned across the subject. This type of radiography is used to determine bone density.[3] It is not used to examine fractures because the images are not clear enough for fractures to be seen. DEXA is very useful for patients suffering from osteoporosis and other bone disorders.

Fluoroscopy is the use of real-time X-ray-generated images to view movement. The modern fluoroscope is an improved version of the early devices scientists used to view X-ray images in real time. Fluoroscopy is used to guide physicians in medical intervention, such as biopsies or placement of pacemakers. It is also used to observe the functioning of body structures as they move.[4] For example, fluoroscopy can be used with the circulatory system to find aneurysms or blockages. As with CT scans, fluoroscopy often relies on a contrast agent to help better visualize soft structures such as blood vessels.

In addition to radiography, X-rays have therapeutic uses, especially for cancer. Beams of X-rays can be directed at

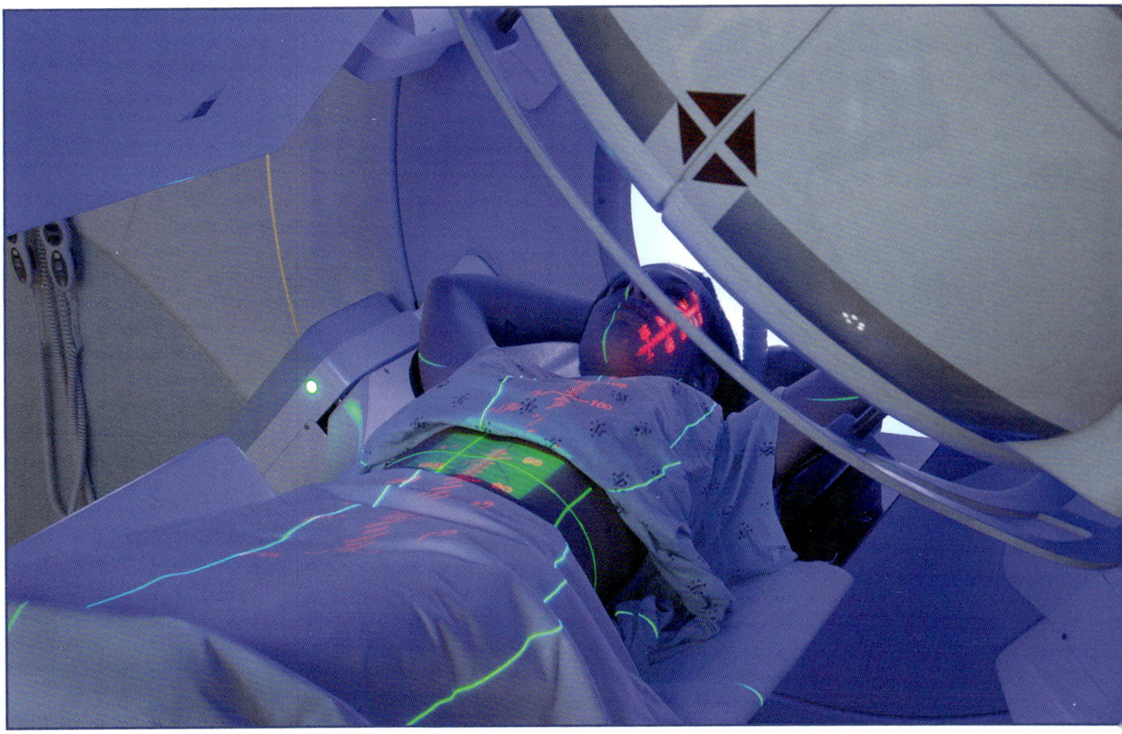

This woman is undergoing radiation treatment for cancer. Beams of X-rays are used to kill cancer cells. These beams can be very focused, so that damage to tissues around the cancer is limited.

tumors. This causes the tumor cells to die, which results in the tumor shrinking or disappearing entirely. Radiation therapy can also kill cancer cells that are beginning to move away from the tumor (metastasizing). This course of therapy is often, but not always, combined with other therapies, such as chemotherapy and surgery.

Limits of Medical X-Rays

Medical X-rays are valuable tools for physicians, yet they are not perfect. Most importantly, ionizing radiation can be harmful to living tissue. Thus, the number of radiography images that a person can be subjected to is limited within a given time frame.

DOSAGE DIFFERENCES

Although standard projection X-ray photographs and CT scans may both use X-rays to generate images of internal structures, the doses for each are very different. For example, the average dose for a chest X-ray is 0.1 millisieverts, while the average dose for a chest CT is 7.0 millisieverts. That's seventy times as much!

The dose from X-ray films is so low that you need not be concerned about having too much exposure. However, anyone who undergoes CT imaging should keep track of their total number of scans. If possible, limit these scans or choose an alternative method to avoid overexposure.

For example, the American College of Radiology suggests that a person should not receive more than twenty-five chest CTs in their life, due to an increased risk of cancer.[5]

As well as long-term exposure problems, high doses of radiation in a short time period can cause acute effects, such as burns. This is often observed with radiation therapy for tumors. These effects must be carefully managed to ensure the patient's quality of life is not compromised too much.

In addition to problems arising from radiation exposure, radiography itself has limitations. Low-density structures, such as muscle, do not show up well on radiography images. This limits the types of conditions these images can be used to investigate. For example, many diseases of soft tissues, such as stomach ulcers and inflammation, cannot be seen using radiography. Other diagnostic procedures are required to ascertain the damage these conditions cause.

Furthermore, X-ray images do not generally show problems such as discoloration, which can be an indicator of the health of tissue. Images may, in addition, be blurry or imprecise, depending on the techniques and tools used. Thus, X-ray images are sometimes combined with other diagnostic tools or are bypassed for more precise methods, depending on the nature of the patient's complaint.

CHAPTER FOUR

HARM FROM X-RAYS

X-rays, being ionizing radiation, have the potential to cause harm to living things, including humans. Thus great care must be taken when using them to ensure they do not cause harm, either in the short or long term.

Health Effects of Radiation

The health effects of radiation vary, but they can be classified in several different ways. The first classification relates to the likelihood any effect will occur. There are two categories: deterministic and stochastic.[1] Deterministic effects depend on dose—the higher the dose, the more the effect will be present. Deterministic effects also have a threshold. Below this minimum dose, these effects do not occur. Stochastic effects, however, have no threshold and do not depend on dose. Rather, they may occur if any dose is received, but the chances of their occurrence increase as dose increases. For example, burns are a deterministic effect of radiation exposure. Below 6.0 sieverts, burns do not occur. As dose increases, the severity of the burn increases. Cancer is a stochastic effect. Radiation exposure of any amount may cause cancer, but higher doses increase the chances cancer will occur.

The second classification relates to the timing of the effects. Acute effects are those that happen shortly after the dose is received. These effects will go away eventually. Acute effects are often also called radiation sickness. Latent effects are those that arise long after exposure.[2] For example, nausea, vomiting, and burns are acute effects, while cataracts and cancer are latent effects.

The third classification relates to who suffers the effects. Somatic effects are those that take place in the individual who

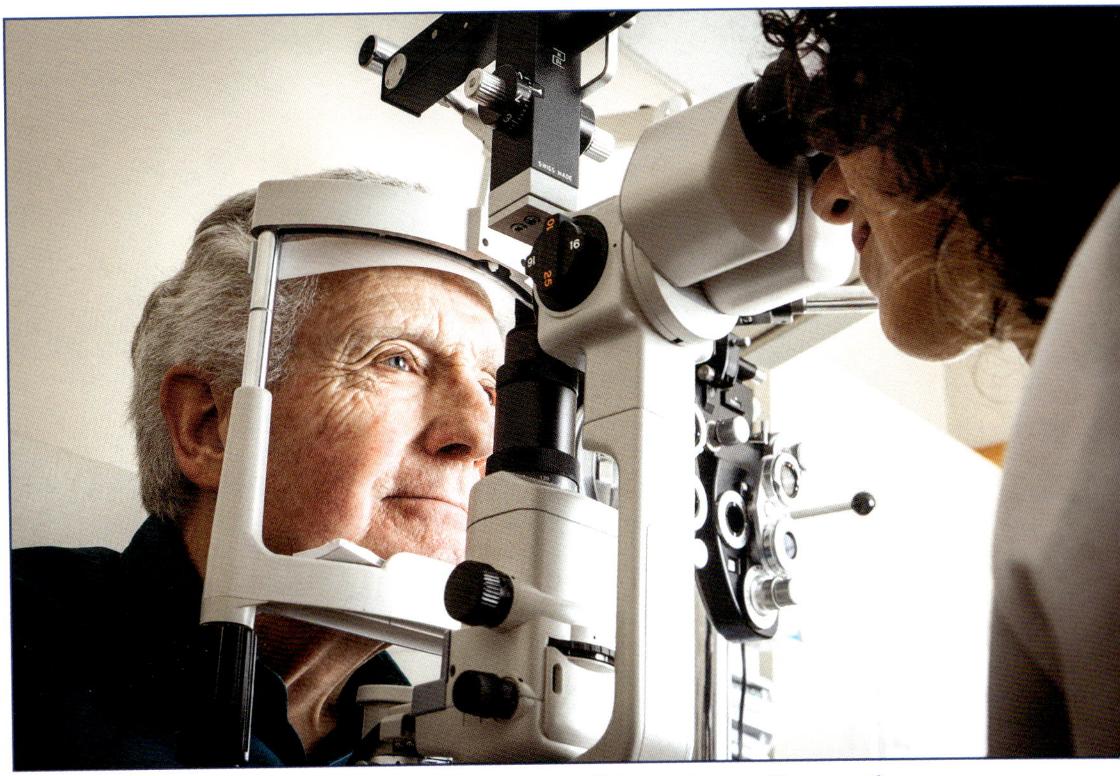

This person has cataracts, a condition that affects the eyes. Cataracts are cloudy films that grow over the lens of the eye. Cataracts can be caused by radiation exposure.

received the exposure. Genetic effects are those that arise in that person's offspring.[3] For example, a person exposed to radiation may have somatic effects such as burns and cancer, while her children may have genetic effects such as birth defects and deformities. Genetic effects may or may not occur, even if a person suffered somatic effects.

Units and Acceptable Limits

There are many different ways of calculating the amount of radiation a person is exposed to. These different units describe either how much radiation is coming from a source, how much radiation is traveling through the air, how much radiation a person is receiving, or how much radiation a person's organs are absorbing. That's a lot of different measurements!

RADIATION SICKNESS

Radiation sickness is the name given to the cluster of symptoms that often arise after large exposures. The common symptoms of radiation sickness are nausea, vomiting, skin burns, and hair loss.

Radiation sickness cannot be cured, but it can be treated. First, the source of the radiation must be removed. Then symptoms are managed. This can include putting salve on burns and using antiemetics to stop vomiting. These treatments only reduce symptoms. They do not reverse the damage done by radiation.

In the United States, the curie (Ci) measures how much radiation is coming from a source. The roentgen (R) measures how much radiation is traveling through the air. The rad measures how much radiation a person receives. The rem measures how much radiation a person's organs absorb.

In the international system (SI), the becquerel (Bq) measures how much radiation is coming from a source. The coulomb/kilogram (C/kg) measures how much radiation is traveling through the air. The gray (Gy) measures how much radiation a person receives. The sievert (Sv) measures how much radiation a person's organs absorb.

The limits of acceptable radiation doses depend greatly on how long the person is exposed. The Nuclear Regulatory Commission (NRC) of the United States sets legal acceptable limits for people who are exposed to radiation sources as part of their jobs. These limits include no more than 5 rems per year for a person's whole body, although extremities such as arms, legs, and fingers can have higher doses. The NRC also limits exposure for members of the general public to 100 millirems (1/10th rem) per year. The general public may also be exposed to no more than 2 millirems per hour from external sources.[4] Importantly, this does not include medical imaging, such as X-rays and CTs.

Doses can be monitored using small devices that absorb X-rays. These devices, called dosimeter badges, are analyzed to determine the amount of radiation they have absorbed. The badges can be affixed to stationary objects, such as walls, to determine how much radiation exists in an area. They can also be worn by people to determine the dose a person has received. They are crucial to keeping people safe from high levels of radiation associated with their jobs. Next time you have an X-ray

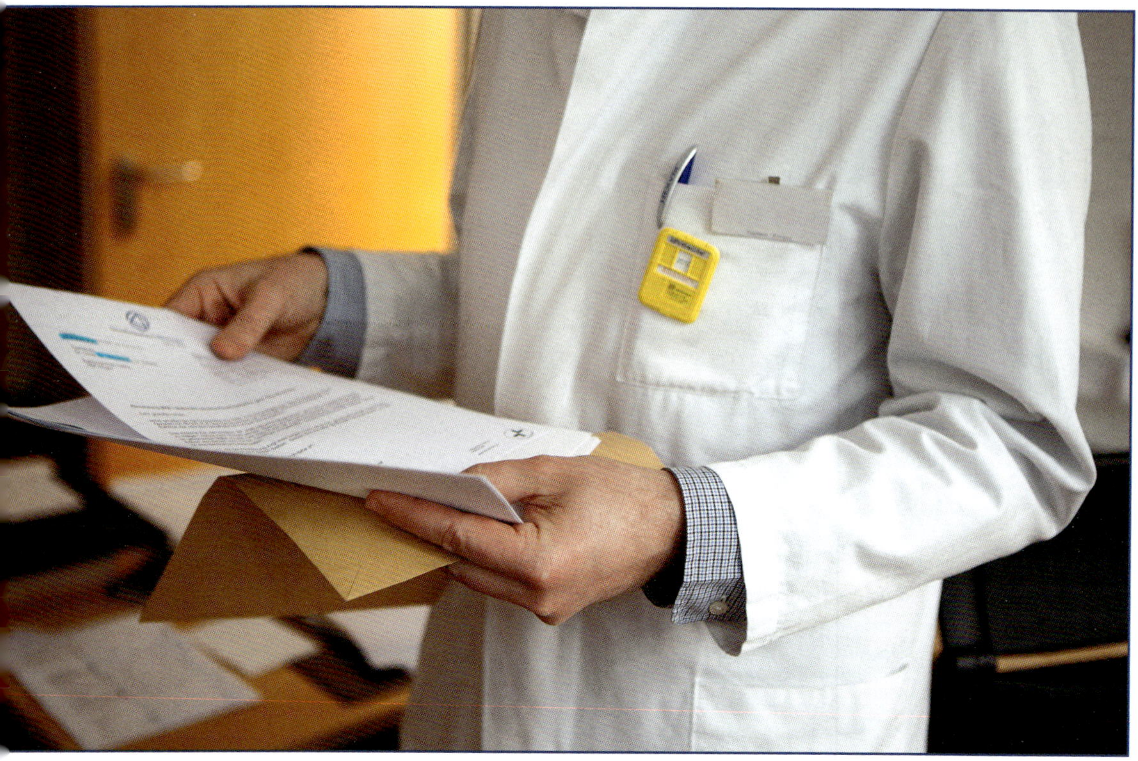

This person is wearing a radiation dosimetry badge. The yellow badge is attached to the pocket of the person's lab coat. This badge helps the person monitor their radiation exposure.

taken, take a moment to look for one of these badges in the room or attached to your X-ray technician's clothing.

Alternatives to Medical X-Rays

X-rays remain one of the best tools physicians have for diagnosing and monitoring health conditions. However, there are alternatives, some of which pose a lower risk to the patient.

Ultrasound devices are often used to generate images of internal structures. These devices use sound waves to generate an image. This is possible because sound waves reflect differently off of surfaces with different densities. Ultrasound technology is commonly used to generate images of developing fetuses because their tissues are too delicate to be imaged with X-rays. But fetal images are not the only use of ultrasounds. They can also be used to generate images of soft tissue organs, such as the heart, bladder, and kidneys. Many physicians use ultrasound devices to guide surgical procedures as well. Like X-rays, ultrasound devices are noninvasive.

Light waves in other wavelength ranges may also be used. All electromagnetic radiation with wavelengths longer than ultraviolet is nonionizing, meaning it is not harmful to living things. Infrared (IR) and terahertz (THz) waves can be used to examine hard and soft tissues, respectively. IR imaging is especially useful for dentists because the teeth are exposed to the air, so the rays do not need to penetrate soft tissues. THz imaging has limited use in medical applications and is more commonly used in security screening, such as airport security checkpoints. This is because THz waves do not pass through the body.

Finally, magnetic resonance imaging (MRI) scans offer many of the advantages of X-ray scans, especially CTs, without the exposure to ionizing radiation. MRIs generate strong magnetic fields and use radio waves to generate an image of body tissues. Similarly to CTs, MRIs can add a contrast agent to help soft structures appear visible on the scans. MRIs have some advantage over CTs in that they can show the amount of blood flow in a particular area. This property makes them especially valuable for brain imaging. MRIs that show varying blood flow to different parts of the brain are called functional MRIs (fMRIs).

CHAPTER FIVE

NUCLEAR WEAPONRY

Medical X-rays have been used to help millions of people. Yet X-rays have a much more nefarious use. X-rays are integral to nuclear bombs. Although opinion is divided on the use of nuclear weapons, the fact remains that these weapons do exist and may again be used one day.

Fission Weapons

The first nuclear weapons developed were fission weapons. They have also been called atom bombs, or A-bombs, but this name is a misnomer because all nuclear weapons rely on atoms, and the relevant portion of the atom involved is the nucleus. These weapons were developed in the late 1930s as World War II began. The first detonation of a nuclear bomb occurred on July 16, 1945, at a test site in Alamagordo, New Mexico.[1]

Fission weapons are those that do damage entirely resulting from nuclear fission—that is, the nuclei of atoms split, causing explosions.

In fact, most of the energy released by a fission weapon is in the form of X-rays. These rays are accompanied by a tremendous amount of heat. The heat generated in a fission explosion reaches temperatures about three times those within the core of our sun.[2] The energy contained in the release of these X-rays is extremely damaging.

Fission weapons rely on radioactive isotopes that undergo rapid decay. These are primarily uranium-235 and plutonium-239. Uranium-233 is sometimes used as well.[3] The number after the name of the element indicates the number of subatomic particles in the nucleus.

Explosion is initiated either by firing an explosive material into the core of the weapon or by compressing it. The first method causes some isotopes to begin to decay, and they in turn fuel even more isotopes to decay, in an exponentially

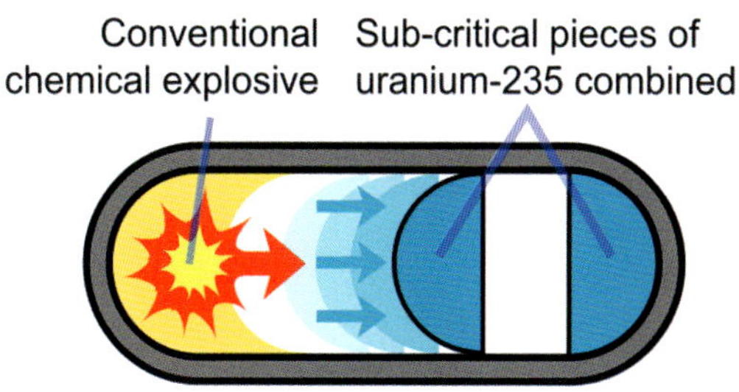

Gun-type assembly method

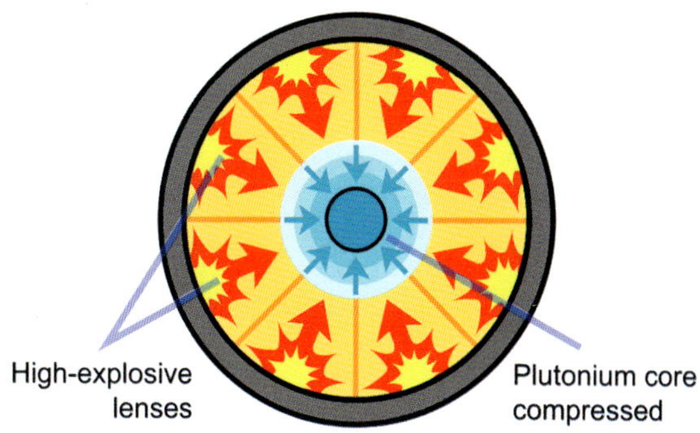

Implosion assembly method

Two explosion methods are used in fission weapons. The gun-type assembly fires an explosive material into radioactive isotopes. The implosion assembly compresses the isotopes until they explode.

greater and greater chain reaction. The second method, called radioactive implosion, causes the energy of the isotopes to rebound off of explosive lenses, which then in turn fuel additional explosions.

Fusion Weapons

Shortly after scientists began investigating fission weapons, they determined that they could harness the energy generated by the initial explosion to power an even larger explosion. These weapons, sometimes called hydrogen bombs, H-bombs, or thermonuclear weapons, undergo two stages: a fission stage and a fusion stage.

The fission stage proceeds exactly like a fission weapon. The same elements are used in the fission core: uranium-235 or plutonium-239.

The fusion stage requires thermonuclear fuel, which is either a radioisotope of hydrogen (deuterium, H-2, or tritium, H-3), or lithium deuteride, a compound containing both lithium and deuterium. The use of heavy hydrogen is where these bombs get the name hydrogen bomb.

The X-rays generated in the fission stage drive the fusion stage of a fusion weapon. The incredible heat and energy of the fission reaction are harnessed and compressed, setting off a series of high-energy reactions in the hydrogen. It is not precisely understood just how these reactions happen, but what is understood is that the total energy output of a fusion weapon is much, much greater than a fission weapon. Whereas fission weapons can only reach about a hundred kilotons, fusion weapons can extend into tens of thousands. This is the equivalent of tens of thousands of metric tons of TNT.

Ethics and Governance

As you might expect, opinion on the use of nuclear weapons is divided. Many people question whether they should even exist at all.

Only twice have nuclear bombs ever been used in combat—once when United States forces dropped a bomb on Hiroshima, Japan, and the other just three days later when United States forces dropped another bomb on Nagasaki, Japan. Tens of thousands of people, mostly civilians, died instantly, and more than a hundred thousand died from radiation exposure and injuries in the following months. These bombings occurred on August 6 and August 9, 1945.[4]

Even before the bombs were dropped, many people had serious concerns about their use. Even those involved in their development had reservations about using them in combat, preferring them to serve as a deterrent rather than an actual act of force.

Because a nuclear explosion cannot avoid killing civilians and causing radioactive damage to both living and nonliving things, many people oppose their use on ethical grounds. The Geneva Convention, a meeting of heads of state that outlines the tenets of humanitarian treatment of people all over the world, forbids the killing of noncombatants, especially those attempting to help the injured during war.[5] The fact that nuclear bombs cannot avoid this sort of killing specifically renders their use forbidden under these tenets.

HIBAKUSHA

***Hibakusha* is the name Japanese people often use to refer to the victims of the nuclear bomb explosions of 1945. The word comes from a combination of Japanese words: *hi*, meaning "affected;" *baku*, meaning "bomb;" and *sha*, meaning "people."**

Many hibakusha have been interviewed to share their stories, and some have even traveled the world, speaking to dignitaries and government officials. They often campaign for disarmament and peace. They give voice to the human toll war can take.

For this reason, many countries ceased all development of nuclear weapons following the 1945 bombings of Japan. However, some countries continued to develop and stockpile nuclear weapons.

Due to the terrible destructive power of nuclear weapons, the 1950s witnessed the Cold War, a nonviolent conflict borne of the mere threat of nuclear bombs. The United States faced off against the Soviet Union, each stockpiling large numbers of nuclear weapons.

By the late 1950s, the United Nations began efforts to deter nuclear weapons development, stockpiling, testing, and use. Heads of state of many countries readily agreed not to develop or use nuclear weapons. However, governments of a few countries have still refused to eliminate nuclear weapons, including the United States.

Those who oppose disarmament point out that any countries that maintain a stockpile of nuclear weapons have a wartime

The stockpiling and use of nuclear weapons is highly controversial. Many people, like these demonstrators, oppose nuclear weapons in all forms.

advantage that cannot be countered. This makes those countries a huge threat. Some people believe nuclear weapon stockpiles must be maintained as a deterrent to any country detonating a nuclear bomb because this act would be swiftly followed by the detonation of a nuclear bomb on that country's own soil. This stalemate is known as mutually assured destruction—if anybody pulls their trigger, everyone loses.

For now, peace is maintained through the agreement of all countries not to detonate nuclear bombs. A few proponents of nuclear weapons see this as a direct result of stockpiles—the threat of nuclear war is great enough to deter smaller-scale aggression. Yet many people disagree with this view, and multiple groups across the globe continue to call for disarmament. But as long as any country maintains stockpiles of nuclear weapons, it is unlikely all other countries will disarm.

CHAPTER SIX

X-RAYS AND SCIENTIFIC DISCOVERY

The most widespread human use of X-rays is medical. Yet that is not their only use. X-rays have many scientific and engineering applications. Aside from their use in nuclear bombs, these applications further discovery and humanity's understanding of the natural world.

X-Ray Astronomy

Astronomical observations were first performed with lenses that simply magnified the visible light emitted by solar objects. As humanity's understanding of electromagnetic radiation deepened, scientists began to understand that cosmic objects give off not only visible light, but also light across the electromagnetic spectrum. The detection of X-rays given off by cosmic objects allows astronomers to detect many objects that would be difficult to see with instruments that only absorb visible light. It also helps astronomers understand more about the objects they can see.

Stars give off X-rays and can be examined with X-ray telescopes. Yet stars are not the only objects that emit X-rays. Whole galaxies, as well as galactic centers, also emit X-rays, as do black holes. Our sun, a star, emits X-rays, which are reflected off every object in our solar system, including our moon. Thus, scientists can examine solar objects by viewing the X-rays reflected off them.[1]

X-ray telescopes can be used to observe and record these emissions and reflections. X-rays explain many things left unexplained by visible light. For example, the X-ray luminosity of a star can indicate the composition and density of distant stars. It can be used to predict where stars might form and to pick out very young stars that are not yet bright enough to be seen in the visible spectrum. It can help scientists find magnetic fields around extrasolar bodies as well, including other stars.[2]

The intricacies of X-ray astronomy are not all well understood yet. Most of the fields of theoretical astronomy and theoretical astrophysics involve sources of X-rays and the manner in which X-rays are emitted. Theoretical, in this sense, does not mean a guess. Rather, it means these fields are based on mathematical observations of the universe and the predictions made by mathematical models. It can be very difficult to observe the data needed to support these theories, so separate fields, applied astronomy and applied astrophysics, deal with making observations. In fact, much of applied astrophysics involves building the necessary tools to make observations that can support or refute the models proposed by theoretical astrophysics. Proper X-ray telescopes are instrumental in this search for data.

ASTRONAUTS AND RADIATION

Space is full of X-rays and other ionizing radiation. Most of it does not reach Earth's surface because Earth's atmosphere reflects it. But NASA engineers must account for this radiation when designing spacecraft and spacesuits.

Most spacecraft are lined with protective shielding. This shielding holds heat inside the craft and keeps most radiation out. However, astronauts still receive higher doses than people on Earth. Astronauts on the International Space Station receive up to 28 millirads per day, while people on Earth only receive less than 2.

Astronauts receive much higher doses of radiation than people on Earth. Spacesuits, spacecraft, and space stations are lined with protective material, but a lot of radiation still gets through.

X-Ray Crystallography

In the early twentieth century, debate raged as to whether X-rays were electromagnetic radiation or something else. In 1922, American physicist Arthur Compton showed that electrons could scatter X-rays, definitively demonstrating these rays were, in fact, light.

But the scattering of X-rays by electrons had another important implication. It meant that crystals could be examined using X-rays.

A crystal is a solid with a regular, repeating structure. The atoms of any crystal have a little bit of space between them, and the regular spacing of the atoms creates a pattern. X-rays striking atoms are like waves striking the posts that hold up a pier. The incoming wave has a certain speed and direction, and when it strikes the posts, they reflect waves out in every direction. These reflected waves precisely show where the posts are. In fact, you could probably point out where the posts are if you could only see the waves. X-ray crystallography works exactly this way.

Most of the X-rays that move toward a crystal pass right through it, but a few strike atoms and are reflected and refracted. Light waves interfere with each other. When they are out of phase, meaning that one wave's crests line up with another wave's troughs, it is destructive interference. The result of destructive interference is a wave with no amplitude—no wave. When they are in phase, meaning that one wave's crests line up with another wave's crests, it is constructive interference. The result of constructive interference is a wave with an amplitude that is the sum of the amplitudes of the original waves.

To determine the atomic structure of a crystal, scientists can use the pattern of interference made by X-rays. The crystal is placed in front of a screen that absorbs X-rays. The beam is passed through the crystal, and the pattern of its diffraction is absorbed on the screen. Bright spots are places that show constructive interference, while dark spots are places that show destructive interference. From this pattern, the shape of the crystal can be calculated.[3]

Scientists must have a thorough understanding of mathematics, especially geometry, in order to solve a crystal structure from a diffraction pattern. This is how the structures of many important molecules, including DNA, were solved.

Anthropology

Anthropology is the study of human cultures and the way they change over time. Anthropologists can use X-rays to help them understand these cultures.

X-rays can be used to examine human remains, especially those within coffins or sarcophagi. Human remains can be delicate, breaking or crumbling if subjected to too much physical damage. X-rays can help anthropologists peer into coffins and sarcophagi to better understand the remains of those entombed inside them. In many cases, the X-ray image of a human skeleton from long ago can reveal the person's age, sex, health, and even cause of death.

Many anthropologists examine artifacts, or the physical objects left behind by humans. These artifacts may be delicate or difficult to move. X-rays can be a valuable technology for studying

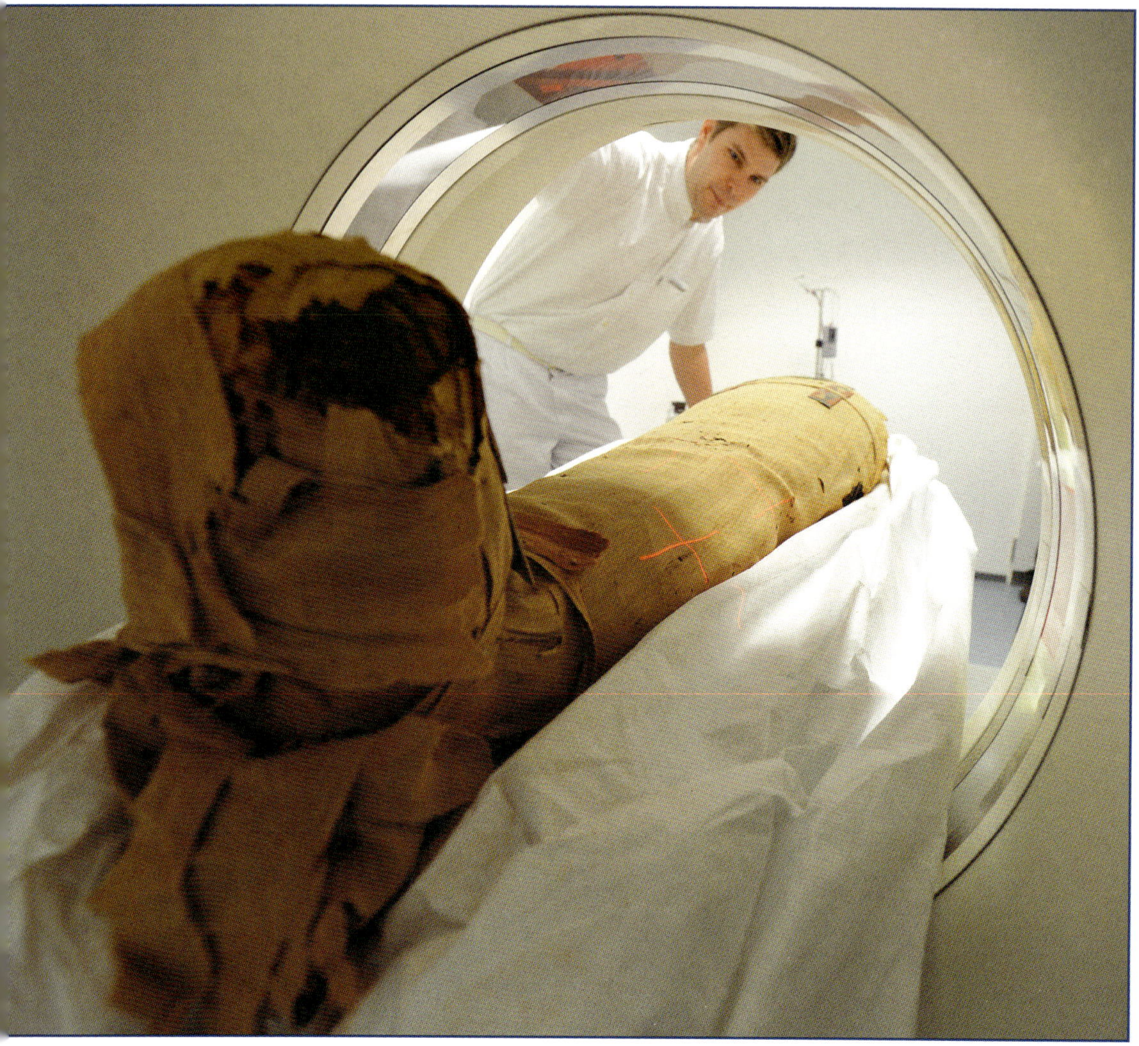

Anthropologists can use the same types of devices doctors use. Here, an anthropologist takes a CT scan of a mummy to study the mummy's internal structures without damaging the mummy.

them. X-rays can help anthropologists determine the materials that make up an artifact. They can also help anthropologists peer inside complex artifacts or those that have been covered over time by soil, ash, or organic matter.

X-rays can also help anthropologists determine whether objects are worth putting in time and effort to recover. Many artifacts and human remains are found buried or in poor condition. They must be unearthed and restored in order to be studied, but this process is costly and takes a long time. X-ray examinations of these artifacts and remains can help anthropologists learn more about the objects so they can decide whether the cost of continuing to study them is worthwhile.

CHAPTER SEVEN

OTHER USES OF X-RAYS

X-rays have many other practical uses. Care must always be taken when using them to ensure the health and safety of everyone around them. However, X-rays are fairly cheap and efficient and provide a valuable technology in many fields. X-rays are especially useful because they do not break or damage the objects they pass through. This is known as the nondestructive property of X-rays.

Security Scanning

Have you ever traveled by plane? When you went to the airport, you had to pass through a security checkpoint. Many of these checkpoints use X-rays to examine items destined for airplanes. X-rays here are used to check for prohibited materials.

There are several types of scanners, only some of which use X-rays. The most common type of X-ray scanner is a cabinet scanner, which is used only to scan luggage, not living things. The luggage passes into the cabinet, usually on a conveyor belt, and the

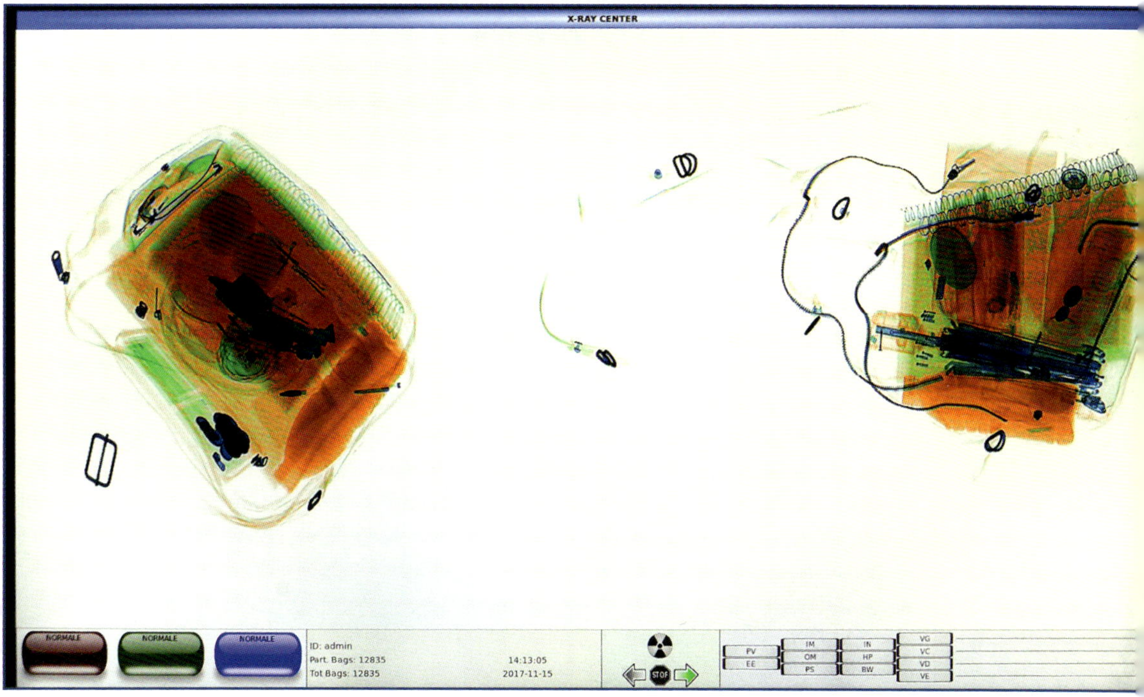

Security screening machines use X-rays to examine the contents of luggage and other containers. Computers add color to images of certain materials to make them easy to spot.

cabinet is then closed. The X-rays are completely contained within the cabinet, ensuring no one in the area is exposed to any radiation.[1]

The image produced by cabinet X-ray scanners is a real-time color image. Different materials show up as different colors, depending on their atomic makeup. This helps security personnel quickly detect prohibited materials. Furthermore, because the scanners use X-rays, security personnel can quickly and easily examine all items in luggage without opening it or going through the packed bag. This speeds up the process for passengers.

Additionally, some X-ray scanners are used to examine passengers. These scanners use a very small dose of radiation and detect the scattering of the X-rays off the person's body. These scanners aren't always used. Some security checkpoints instead use metal detectors, which use magnets to detect metal objects. Increasingly, millimeter wave detectors are being used at security checkpoints. These detectors use radio waves to examine individuals. Radio waves are not ionizing radiation, so this method is far safer than X-ray scanners. The waves used in millimeter wave detectors do not pass through a person's body—they bounce off the surface, just as visible light does.

Counterfeit Detection

The electronics industry is vital to the economies of many countries. People all over the world rely on electronics daily. Electronics are in cell phones, televisions, laptops, cars, and even kitchen appliances.

The demand for electronics is very high, which means the demand for the parts needed to build those electronics is also very high. Unfortunately, this high demand leads to an opportunity for dishonest dealers—counterfeit electronic parts.

The capacitors, resistors, switches, semiconductors, and circuit boards needed to build electronics are not always readily available. This creates an opportunity for counterfeiters to replace good parts with fake ones. These counterfeit parts may be made out of bad materials or may not be manufactured properly. At best, counterfeit parts cause electronics to run inefficiently or malfunction. At worst, they can lead to dangerous breakdowns of electronics. This can hurt users and be very costly for manufacturers.

X-rays are an important tool in the detection of counterfeit electronic components. The use of inferior materials is difficult to see with the naked eye, even using a microscope. X-rays, however, reflect differently off of different materials. In this way, they can clearly indicate when inferior materials have been used to manufacture a part.

In addition, many electronic components are sealed, and opening them would destroy them. X-rays can be used to peer inside these components without damaging them. This allows inspectors to ensure they are properly made and to catch any badly made parts before they are installed.[2]

Electronics are not the only counterfeits that X-rays can detect. X-rays are also used to detect art forgeries. For paintings, X-rays can reveal what lies hidden beneath the paint without harming the canvas. Some forgers use canvases made after the time period in which the painting is known to have been made. These forgeries can be detected with X-rays, which can find the canvas layer beneath the paint. The interior parts of sculptures can also be examined to check for nails or resins that may give away the forgery. Of course, many other detection methods are also required to detect art forgeries.[3]

X-rays can also be used to detect counterfeit money. In a manner similar to the detection of inferior electronics materials, the material in bank notes can be scanned with X-rays to determine its chemical makeup. If the chemicals used to make the bank note do not match those in verified bank notes, the money is clearly counterfeit. X-rays are just one tool used in counterfeit money detection.[4]

MASTERPIECES OVER MASTERPIECES

Art forgeries are common, but so are hidden masterpieces. Many paintings are exactly as they appear to be. But sometimes an artist made part of a painting, or even a whole painting, and then covered it up with a different painting.

In fact, in 2008, art scientists uncovered a painting underneath "Patch of Grass" by Vincent van Gogh. Underneath the painting of grass and wildflowers, X-rays revealed a portrait of a person. No one knows who this person was, or why van Gogh painted over the portrait.

This painting by Vincent van Gogh is painted over another painting. X-rays revealed a portrait beneath the painting of grass.

Public Safety and Other Uses

An important use of X-rays is food safety. X-rays are used to kill harmful bacteria and mold on the surfaces of foods, especially fruits and vegetables. This keeps foods fresher longer and helps protect people from food poisoning. While the X-rays kill bacteria and mold, they do not damage the food at all. Foods that have been treated with X-rays are safe to eat.

Because X-rays can help people peer inside objects without damaging them, they have many useful applications in engineering, design, and manufacturing. For example, X-rays can be used to examine the structural integrity of bridges, railroads, pipelines, and buildings. They can also be used to examine the parts of airplanes, spacecraft, train cars, and vehicles. This helps engineers ensure parts are made correctly with no defects and fit together properly. They can also be used to find breaks or cracks in existing infrastructure so only damaged parts can be repaired rather than replacing entire systems. This nondestructive testing helps guarantee the safety of the public, who will be using the objects in everyday life. Manufacturers also use X-rays to inspect parts as they are made. X-rays can find small holes, breaks, or deformities in manufactured parts. These parts may be electronic components, vehicle parts, and safety equipment.

X-rays are also useful in geology. X-rays are absorbed and reflected differently on different surfaces, including different mineral deposits in rocks. This allows geologists to examine rocks for certain minerals without completely destroying them. This helps geologists find important deposits of natural resources, such as metal ores, salts, oil, and coal. It can also help scientists gain a better understanding of the makeup of Earth's crust. It

X-rays can be used to examine infrastructure for problems. Here, an X-ray machine (the blue box) is used to examine a pipeline.

further allows scientists to understand and predict tectonic plate movement—the movement of the large pieces of Earth's crust that overlap, crash into one another, and move apart.[5]

X-rays have great power for helping people, but they also have great power for harm. The use of X-rays has allowed many people to live happy, healthy lives and has helped ensure the safety of many others. Yet X-rays have also been integral to the development of nuclear weapons, some of the most destructive objects ever developed by humans. Clearly, X-rays require responsible use and careful consideration of their effects.

CHAPTER NOTES

CHAPTER 1
THE ELECTROMAGNETIC SPECTRUM

1. *Encyclopedia Britannica*, online ed., s.v. "X-ray."

CHAPTER 2
THE HISTORY OF X-RAYS

1. Alexi Assmus, "Early History of X-Rays," *Stanford Beam Line*, vol. 25, issue 2, pp. 10–24, http://www.slac.stanford.edu/pubs/beamline/25/2/25-2-assmus.pdf (accessed March 12, 2019).
2. "Wilhelm Conrad Röntgen—Facts," Nobel Media AB 2019, https://www.nobelprize.org/prizes/physics/1901/rontgen/lecture (accessed March 12, 2019).
3. Gilbert King, "Clarence Dally—The Man Who Gave Thomas Edison X-Ray Vision," *Smithsonian*, March 4, 2012, https://www.smithsonianmag.com/history/clarence-dally-the-man-who-gave-thomas-edison-x-ray-vision-123713565/#hW1XITGwQiuhzgzu.99 (accessed March 12, 2019).
4. *Encyclopedia Britannica*, online ed., s.v. "Mihajlo Pupin."

CHAPTER 3
MEDICAL USES OF X-RAYS

1. Albert L. Baert, *Encyclopedia of Imaging, Vol. 2.* (New York, NY: Springer, 2008), p. 322.
2. *Encyclopedia Britannica*, online ed., s.v. "Computed Tomography."

3. "Dual Energy X ray Absorptiometry—Bone Mineral Densitometry," International Atomic Energy Agency, August 7, 2017, https://www.iaea.org/resources/rpop/health-professionals/other-specialities-and-imaging-modalities/dxa-bone-mineral-densitometry (accessed March 13, 2019).
4. "Fluoroscopy Procedure." Johns Hopkins Medicine Health Library, https://www.hopkinsmedicine.org/healthlibrary/test_procedures/orthopaedic/fluoroscopy_procedure_92,p07662 (accessed March 13, 2019).
5. *ACR–AAPM–SPR Practice Parameter for Diagnostic Reference Levels and Achievable Doses in Medical X-Ray Imaging,* American College of Radiography, updated 2018.

CHAPTER 4

HARM FROM X-RAYS

1. *IARC Monographs on the Evaluation of Carcinogenic Risks to Humans, No. 75*, IARC Working Group on the Evaluation of Carcinogenic Risk to Humans (Lyon, France: International Agency for Research on Cancer, 2000).
2. *IARC Monographs on the Evaluation of Carcinogenic Risks to Humans.*
3. *IARC Monographs on the Evaluation of Carcinogenic Risks to Humans.*
4. *Dose Standards and Methods for Protection Against Radiation and Contamination*, Rev 0603, United States Nuclear Regulatory Commission, sec. 8-2.

CHAPTER 5

NUCLEAR WEAPONRY

1. "The First Atomic Bomb Test Is Successfully Exploded," History.com, https://www.history.com/this-day-in-history/the-first-atomic-bomb-test-is-successfully-exploded (accessed March 14, 2019).
2. "Hydrogen Bomb—1950," Atomic Heritage Foundation, https://www.atomicheritage.org/history/hydrogen-bomb-1950 (accessed March 15, 2019).
3. "How Do Nuclear Weapons Work?" Union of Concerned Scientists, https://www.ucsusa.org/nuclear-weapons/how-do-nuclear-weapons-work (accessed March 15, 2019).
4. *Encyclopedia Britannica*, online ed., s.v. "Hiroshima and Nagasaki."
5. "Geneva IV," *Geneva Convention Relative to the Protection of Civilian Persons in Times of War*, United Nations Treaty Series, articles 13–24.

CHAPTER 6

X-RAYS AND SCIENTIFIC DISCOVERY

1. *Encyclopedia Britannica*, online ed., s.v. "X-ray Astronomy."
2. E. J. Gaidos, "Nearby Young Solar Analogs, I. Catalog and Stellar Characteristics," *Publications of the Astronomical Society of the Pacific*, 110 (753): 1259–76.
3. M. S. Smyth and J.H.J. Martin, "X Ray Crystallography," Molecular Pathology, 2000 Feb; 53(1): 8–14.

CHAPTER 7

OTHER USES OF X-RAYS

1. "Radiation and Airport Security Scanning," United States Environmental Protection Agency, https://www3.epa.gov/radtown/airport-security-scanning.html (accessed March 20, 2019).
2. Art Ogg, "Using X-ray to Detect Counterfeit Components," Circuit Insight, http://www.circuitinsight.com/programs/51457.html (accessed March 21, 2019).
3. "Using Science to Detect Art Forgeries," University of Glasgow: Future Learn, https://www.futurelearn.com/courses/art-crime/0/steps/11884 (accessed March 21, 2019).
4. Jennifer Caban, "Money for Nothing: How XRF Helps Solve the Dire Straits of Counterfeit Currency," Olympus: Insight Blog, September 6, 2018, https://www.olympus-ims.com/en/insight/money-for-nothing-how-xrf-helps-solve-the-dire-straits-of-counterfeit-currency.
5. Tim McKenna, "Non Medical Radiography," LinkedIn SlideShare, February 19, 2013, https://www.slideshare.net/tmckenna99/non-medical-radiography (accessed March 22, 2019).

GLOSSARY

ACUTE EFFECTS Radiation exposure effects that happen soon after exposure.

COMPUTED TOMOGRAPHY (CT) X-ray imaging technique that uses a computer along with a beam of X-rays to produce a cross-sectional image of body structures.

DETERMINISTIC EFFECTS Radiation exposure effects that depend on dose, which must surpass a threshold in order to occur.

ELECTROMAGNETIC RADIATION A form of energy without mass that behaves as both a wave and a particle; also called light.

FISSION WEAPON (ATOM BOMB, A-BOMB) A nuclear weapon that uses X-rays to deal damage entirely resulting from nuclear fission.

FLUOROSCOPY The use of real-time X-ray-generated images to view movement.

FUSION WEAPON (HYDROGEN BOMB, H-BOMB) A nuclear weapon that uses X-rays to deal damage through a nuclear fission stage followed by a hydrogen fusion stage.

GENETIC EFFECTS Radiation exposure effects that affect the future children or other descendants of the exposed individual.

IONIZING RADIATION Radiation that can cause electrons to be ejected from matter when it strikes that matter's surface.

LATENT EFFECTS Radiation exposure effects that happen long after exposure.

PROJECTION RADIOGRAPHY The use of X-rays to produce a single two-dimensional image.

RADIOGRAPHY The use of X-rays or other radioactive materials to produce images.

SOMATIC EFFECTS Radiation exposure effects that affect the exposed individual.

STOCHASTIC EFFECTS Radiation exposure effects that do not have a threshold for occurrence, but the chances of occurrence increase with increasing dose.

X-RAY CRYSTALLOGRAPHY The use of the scattering of X-rays by atoms in a crystal to determine the structure of the crystal.

FURTHER READING

BOOKS

Adair, Luther B., and Seth Crapp. *Learning About X-Rays with Lula and Ethan.* San Francisco, CA: Blurb, 2018.

Cooper, Christopher. *The Basics of Nuclear Physics.* New York, NY: Rosen Publishing, 2015.

Hall, Wendy J., and Ysha Morco. *Andy's X-Ray: Mediwonderland.* CreateSpace Independent Publishing Platform, 2017.

Porterfield, Jason. *Jump-Starting a Career in Radiology.* New York, NY: Rosen, 2019.

Wojtan, Nick. *Oops! They're X-rays!* New York, NY: Gareth Stevens Publishing, 2019.

WEBSITES

Britannica Kids: X-Rays

kids.britannica.com/kids/article/X-rays/353941

A kid-friendly version of the *Encyclopedia Britannica* with interactive and read-aloud text.

Curious Kids: How Do X-Rays See Inside You?

theconversation.com/curious-kids-how-do-x-rays-see-inside-you-85895

An informative article with embedded video that discusses X-ray technology. Part of a science journalism for kids series.

Imagine the Universe! X-Ray Astronomy

imagine.gsfc.nasa.gov/science/toolbox/xray_astronomy1.html

A NASA children's outreach and education site with information on NASA's use of X-rays in astronomy.

INDEX